This All Sounded Better in My Head

Idalias Palmer

BookLeaf Publishing

Presentation by *BookLeaf Publishing*

Web: www.bookleafpub.com

E-mail: info@bookleafpub.com

ISBN: 9789357441353

First edition 2023

DEDICATION

To my husband, for always cheering me on. To my daughter, for being an inspiration and main source of my happiness. And to my family, for always knowing I had this in me.

Waves

I belong in the water, you know?
Flowing in the waves.
Carefree and weight-free.
I belong in the water, you know?
Where I can go underneath and tune out the
harsh song of this world.
Where I can float above the surface and feel the
sun on my face.
I belong in the water, you know?
My place of refuge. Even if the closest I can get
to a satisfying plunge is a lukewarm shower.
My place of peace. Even if I have to simulate the
waves with a playlist.
I'm never really far from it.
I belong in the water, you know?

Tethered

Is it possible to care too much?
Sometimes I fear that I do.
I cry at the thought of another being in pain.
I wince when I see others hurting.
I try to help carry others' burdens when I see the
weight is simply too much.
But I also smile when others smile.
I feel like I'm on top of the world when those
around me are happy.
I glow when others are successful.
I feel everything.
Every emotion.
Every laugh.
Every tear.
I feel it.
I'm connected to this world in a way that I will
never understand.
I'm not sure I want to understand.

Delicate

Like a flower,
My heart as delicate as those satin petals…
Yet stronger than those prickly thorns…
DON'T let my delicacy distract you from my
strength.
DON'T let the beautiful colors of my soul
overshadow the tough exterior created to protect it.

Delicate is not synonymous with helpless.
I'm gentle but I'm not weak.

Scared To Think

I'm scared to think it because what if it happens?
What if I accidentally manifest the end of the world?
The death of a friend?
A terrible accident?
The worst day in the history of bad days?
What if I misspeak in my manifestation and conjure
up the wrong thing?
Why does the blessing of powerful manifestation
capabilities sometimes feel like a curse that I'm
afraid to rouse.

Embrace

Tucked in the welcoming nook under your chin,
it's a perfect fit, as if our bodies were two puzzle
pieces...indubitably meant to fit together.
So precise.
Held in the tight embrace of your arms.
Your hand on the center of my back. Comforting me.
Holding me.
Protecting me.
Doing so without a second thought…
It's instinctual at this point.
My legs in between the soft padding of yours.
They're longer than mine by far but that just makes
me luckier - every inch of my legs can get covered by
yours.
It's the perfect amount of warmth.
It's the perfect amount of you
Our heartbeats.
Rhythmically in sync.
This doesn't happen every fime, but when it does, I
can't help but close my eyes and listen intently.
Our bodies subconsciously working together to keep
us going.
Individually and congruently.
Your soft kisses on my forehead. Often lingering,
almost as if to say,
"I know you're still awake in that head of yours - it's
okay to relax now."

The kisses are sleepily executed. But I swear I
wouldn't want them any other way.
The mumbled "I love you" or "I love you too."
Saying it is almost like a reflex now, but I promise
you, I know that you mean it no matter how many
times you say it. Even when you say it half asleep.
This tangle of body parts, this abstract representation
of love, this familiar sequence of adjusting until we're
just right.
It's telling of so many things.
It's representative of so many emotions and feelings.
But to me, it's telling me that my three main needs
are being met:
I am safe.
I am comfortable.
I am so loved by you.
Because it's so familiar to us, it's easy to forget that
this is a silent masterpiece, it's complex parts unique
to us, and us only.
It's beautiful.

Magician

You never told me your trick.
How you were able to captivate me so easily.
We were so so young, but somehow, I still knew
you were the one for me.
We grew up together.
14 and 15.
Now in our twenties, chasing our wildest
dreams.
You are the reason I believe that dreams come
true.
I dreamt and dreamt, and was lucky enough to
get you.
We've experienced the world's highest of highs,
and the enemy's lowest of lows.
Each experience, genuinely making our love
rapidly grow.
I'm so proud of you. I'm so proud of what we've
done already.
We'll lean on each other - let's keep this
progress steady.

What do you think our 14 and 15 year old selves
would say if they saw us now?

Homesick

The phrase "home is wherever I'm with you,"
couldn't be more true.
Across the country, away from me, all I want is
you.
As soon as I'm in your presence, I know I am
okay.
I think I'm home.
You hug me.
I know I'm home.
You kiss me.
I never want to be away from home again.
You hold me tight.
My God, I've been so homesick without you.

Bathroom Floor

Here I am...
On the bathroom floor.
My breath has escaped me.
The walls are closing in rapidly.
I'm sweaty.
My vision blurred.
I came in here to keep this part of me away from
you.
You don't deserve this.
You don't deserve to be with someone who can't
even control the emotions she feels.
You don't deserve to be with someone who feels
everything so strongly that it sometimes
paralyzes her.
You deserve stability.
Here I am...
On the bathroom floor.
You come in.
Why?
Why the hell did you have to come in here?
I don't want you to see me like this.
You cannot see me like this.
You don't deserve a partner that doesn't have her
shit together.

You don't deserve a partner that has so many
problems.
You don't deserve this.
Here I am...
On the bathroom floor.
In your arms.
Warm.
My breathing has slowed down.
How did that happen?
My body isn't stiff anymore.
What is going on?
My deep sobs, now shallow and slow.
How are you doing this?
Here I am...
In our bed.
You're gently holding me.
You're so gentle with me.
I don't deserve this.
I don't deserve you.
But no matter how many times I try to hide it
from you...
There you are...
On the bathroom floor with me.
Telling me that I'm going to be okay. That we're
going to figure this out. That we're going to get
through this.
We. Us. Our.
So here I am...
In our bed.

Where I belong. With you.
I deserve you.
I deserve us.

Orion's Belt

The perfect alignment
of every good thing in us.
Each star in you,
beautifully and carefully crafted.
You shine brighter than anything I've ever
known.
I never knew that I could hold the beauty of the
stars in space, in the palms of my hands.
Yet, here you are.
You are my favorite constellation.

Wedding Bells

13

I often get asked if we're planning on doing a
ceremony because we never did…
But now that she's here, a big ceremony with a
white dress and flowers doesn't really matter to
me anymore.
There's genuinely no declaration of love that we
could share in a ceremony that would even come
close to our shared declaration that we made
together.
She's the ultimate "I love you"
She's the ultimate "for better or for worse"
She's the ultimate "I trust you"
She's the ultimate "we're in this together"
It doesn't get better than that.

Cotton Candy

It's fitting that my first craving was cotton
candy.
A snack made of pure sugar.
It must have been foreshadowing of the
sweetness that was to come from you.

Time Travel

15

I never believed in time travel until I met you.
You've made months turn to weeks, weeks turn
to days, and days turn to hours.
I blink and another week has passed.
I go to sleep and wake up in a new month.
How is it that someone so tiny, is so capable of
altering time and space?
I hope that when you're older, you figure out
how to make time slow down.
I want to enjoy each and every second with you.

Solar System

(I wrote this poem in 2019 - a while before our sweet girl made her arrival. Every word still holds true.)

She's there…in my mind
I can see her face
I can hear her cry
I can feel her small hands
The world may not revolve around Orion's Belt
But trust me…
I will

J.

My first true memory is your birth…
which means I only really know life with you.
My first best friend.
Even when we're apart,
we don't stay apart for long.
Even when I think my thoughts and ideas are
mine, and mine only, you say them aloud.
I guess it's a connection that only siblings can
understand.
I still see you as small and curious.
I don't know if I'll ever see you differently.
But just because I see you as small and curious,
doesn't mean I don't "see" you.
I see your smarts. Your wits. Your charisma.
Your caring nature. Your pure heart.
I see you.

R.

I've heard that a daughter is often a mirror of her
father
This might be true
I'm brave
I'm smart
I'm adventurous
I'm strong
I'm full of love
I'm curious about the world around me.
I'm in touch with nature
I'm savvy
I'm funny
…just like you.

D.

I've never really known you like I do right now.
Now that I'm a mom…I understand a whole lot
more.
I understand the sacrifices you made for us.
The long days, and even longer nights.
I understand why you still check on us before
you go to bed.
I understand the unexplainable bond between a
mother and her babies.
I understand.

Nightmare

That nightmare.
It revealed it all.
Young Idalias' biggest fear.
To be ignored. Left alone. Not a single ear
wanting to hear.
I was holding on tight.
The cliff below me, so scary and so deep.
In front of me, laid an audience…why are they
ignoring me?
I begged.
I cried.
I pleaded.
I screamed with all my might.
But not a single person looked up.
Nobody dared to take in the sight.
Below me, alligators circled.
The chomped their greedy jaws.
Above, I clung on.
No spectator around tried to acknowledge my
calls.
Young Idalias.
If only you knew, how far your voice would
travel.
You're going to get older and before you know
it, the world will be yours to unravel.

You'll have a voice.
You'll use it, I swear.
Those around you will listen, I promise
you…they'll care.
Your heart is your strength.
Your voice is your power.
Your love, as beautiful as a rare flower.
Hold your head up with pride.
Don't let these nightmares get you down.
No matter what's going on around you.
Don't ever let them see you falter or frown.

Baggage Check

Sometimes when my baggage gets too heavy to
carry, I want to hand it to somebody.
But I can't.
I can't burden anyone else with those feelings.
How unfair would that be for them?
To be stuck, listening to rant after rant.
I'm stuck with secrets that only myself and my
walls know.
I'm stuck with secrets that, if shared, would
make others truly reap what they sow.
Sometimes the baggage gets so heavy, that I
have to take it off and let it sit to the side for a
bit.
But I can't let it sit for too long because
somebody might try to open things...try to really
mess with it.
I'm stuck with this baggage, some of it isn't even
mine.
I'm carrying the burdens of others.
Don't worry, I'm fine.
I'll listen to your problems.
Try to curate the perfect thing to say.
I'll comfort you while you cry.
I'll hold onto your baggage so you can have a
better day.

But now my back really hurts.
I'm honestly tired as hell.
My shoulders ache and my joints crack.
I really don't feel so well.
So consider this my baggage check.
I'm setting it all down.
I'm putting it all in a pile.
Walking away without a single extra pound.

Her Home

You were her home for around 284 days.
You were the only thing she knew for that time.
You kept her safe.
You kept her healthy.
You helped her grow and prepare for this world.
And now she's here.
You're still her home.
You still help her grow - you, and solely you, are
responsible for each and every single one of
those rolls in her thighs
You still keep her comfortable - sometimes
simply laying against you soothes her
You still keep her safe - she knows that in your
arms, nothing in this world can hurt her
And for that, I thank you.
I thank every single stretch mark.
I thank every day of fatigue.
I thank every tinge of back pain.
I thank you for all of it.
Because I know that each and every single piece
of this was a contributor for giving us our
constellation.
I would do it a million times over if I had to.
I would.

Postpartum

I love you more than I've ever loved anything.
But when your eyes are closed
And the room is quiet
Dimly lit by the blue hue of your nightlight
Why is it that in those moments…
I crumble?
Why is it that in those moments…
I feel small
I feel scared
I feel unworthy of your love
Why is it that in those moments…
I hyper analyze everything
I fear for things that won't happen
But what if they do?
Why is it that in those moments…
I go from the smiling mom I was
To a mascara streaked mess
Clinging onto my pillow so that I can muffle my
breathing
So that I can try to talk myself out of a panic
attack
So that I don't wake you up from your peaceful
slumber
Why is it that when your eyes open…
I'm fine

You're my focus
You're my happiness
I have no more tears of pain, only those of
happiness
Why is it that when your eye are open…
I forget to ask for help
God, I need help

Through the Looking Glass

27

I wish I saw myself the same way that everyone
else seems to.
My husband thinks I'm caring.
My parents think I'm smart.
My brother thinks I'm organized.
My friends think I have my life together.
Even my therapist seems to think I'm a fantastic
person.
What do I think?
I simply don't think.